Disaster Relief Poems

WPC-Minimal Press
Hanover, NH

Copyright © 2002 Brett Axel
First Printing
First Edition
March 11, 2002

Disaster Relief Poems

"There are souls who find spiritual fulfilment in devising evil."
— Wilhelm Reich

I have fought believing this
all of my life
and all of my life, it seems,
has been fighting to teach it to me.
— Brett Axel

Jaime

Everyone has a disaster.
You were mine.

Contents

Disaster Relief 7
Change of Plan 8
Building Fire 9
The Poetry 10
The Art 11
Seeking Divine Prophets 12
Black 14
Lot 18
New York 19
Trophy Case 20
Juice 21
Pythonic 22
Nostradamus 23
Our Souls 24
Being Safe 25
First Show After 26
Tension 27
World Trade Center 28
Prowl 33
OK 34
High Time I Say 35
Rebecca and the Trees 36
Symbols 37
Portrait of a Girl With a Violin 39
Senses 40
Rack of Postcards 41
Posters of the Lost 42
Rilke's City 44
Choices 46
For a Book 47
My Disaster Poem Book 48
On Leaving New York 49
Your Poem Somewhere 51
Childhood 52

Recovery...53
Rethinking the Crack About Calling
You a Brat, Selena a Drunk and
Melisa the Chupacabra....................................54
Before Children..55
A Plane..57
Board Games...58
Insomnia...59
Self-Examination...60
The Television Will Not Be Revolutionized........62
Money Matters...64
The Pentagon..65
End of Hope...66
The Salamanders..67
Patriotism...69
Constants...70
Van Gogh...71
The Sight..72
I Could, Easy...73
Yes..74
Love Doesn't Die..75
Progress...76
For the "Terrorists"...77
Concession..78

Disaster Relief

When abruptly surrounded by catastrophe
it seems to matter that you feed yourself,
not to prepare a nice meal
that appeals to your taste.
The disappointments of love
become trifling. Language reverts
to it's most basic: instrument
of communication; Paint identifies
hot and cool zones; legs run.
We forsake the reasons
it is good to be alive.

Regaining our hearts has got to be
an important effort
if we are to recover, and that
is the artists' function. So help them.

Dig from the metaphorical debris
with the same intensity
the physical disaster site is penetrated;
locate and rescue our dances,
our paintings, our poetry. If you fail,
there will be little difference
between those who survived
and those who perished
and that will be
the terrorists' preeminent success.

Change of Plan

Timid Iowa girl
Deer in headlights
Overwhelmed by New York
Ready to run home
Even before
Skyscrapers
Come crashing down.

Building Fire

A clearing in the woods
became the perfect site
for a fire under the night's
morbidly beautiful sky.
No planes in the air.
So quiet and twinkly
like the stars were singing.

The Poetry

So many poems
to be written —
Will all of them together
do as much good
As this terrible incident
Has done harm?

The Art

drive a nail into the pupil
of one of your eyes —
become able to see art
everywhere you look.

Seeking Divine Prophets

Once, I lived in the soul of my mother
like being layered with silk scarves.
I wanted to venture out.
To hire myself
as a fisher of divination,
which I did early on, not missing
the comfort or the sadness
of anything I forsook.

At work, love fell on my shoulders
like soot, it's odor
clung to my hair
even after a thorough washing
with peppermint
until I was only my hand
in the moment of it's glide
across a leaf of paper —

figure skater cutting into the ice
to spray an audience
entirely for the spectacle of it
oblivious to the difference
between cheering and shouting,
 oblivious to the divine
buried under the weight
of a crowd's noise.

At work too, I discovered
that there are people
with prophetic words
who are not prophets at all,
but bastards

who say great things
for the most
atrocious of reasons

and this was not
a discovery I took well to.

The little boy in me started to cry.
The mother in me came running
to my little boy's rescue,
saying: *you don't
have to keep doing this.*
With that, in mind, I fired myself
though I continue in my free time
to work as a fisher of divination.
I know now it is a pursuit
better suited to surprises
than expectations.

I have not retreated to live
layered with silk scarves
in the soul of my mother
though I find myself lately
thinking of only that as my home.

Black

What a black day this is.
The sky and the ground
are black. The ocean
off Rockaway beach
is black as far
as the eye can't see.

The Sports Utility Vehicles
that pollute needlessly
250 to 400 times
more than a car
are black. The buses
bringing children to school
are black. The Path train
is black all the way
to Newark New Jersey.

The Cube at Astor
Place is black. No one
is trying to spin it
and, if someone was,
they would be black.
The shops on West 4th Street
are black. The screens
in luxuriously big theaters
are black. In Show World
near the Port
Authority Bus Station
(which, by the way,
is black)
You can put a black quarter
into a black slot

and masturbate
to 90 seconds of blackness.

The USA Today at the Hudson
News Stand is black.
The old woman
behind the counter
at the Krispy Kreme, the one
that usually smiles at you,
with long black hair: she's black.
The Disney Stores are black.
(Even the ones
in the Suburbs).
Popeye's chicken is black
and so are all of the
red beans and rice inside.

A goose suddenly flying
out sync with the formation is black.

The black sheep
that once stood out
From the other sheep
can't be told
from the rest
of the flock now
because all
of the sheep are black.

The Christians are black.
The Wiccans are black.
The Muslims and
the Jews are black.

The politicians telling everyone
to go back to work
and continue to buy
things they don't need at malls.

Everyone who listens
to the politicians
Everyone who believes them
and everyone who says
they are as full of shit
as they were before
patriotism fell from the sky.

Black.

Everyone who thinks
a flag in their window
or on their car
is going to make
an iota of difference.

Every fireman's face,
the living and the dead.
The ambulances
coming and going.
The EMT that wrote
an e-mail to tell me
that took a moment
for them to figure out
that the popping sounds
they were hearing
from inside the building
that just collapsed
were the bullets
of police officers
still trapped inside.

The heat from the fire
burning them alive
was setting off
their ammunition.

Every pit in which
anyone's hope
has fallen in and been lost.

All of them black.

There is a great deal
of blackness. Plenty
to go around.
And it is sure
to get blacker
As the day
turns into night.

Lot

Running from the Trade Center
Running to what feels
Like a safe distance
Not looking back
One of those entire towers
Could come down
Running to — this must be
A safe distance.
Don't stop and look back yet.
Lot's wife's story
Is given to us to be
A bad example.
Still running.
Hearing, is that the buildings
Actually falling?
Even running I didn't really think
It would happen.
It is: can feel the heat and debris
On the back of your neck.

New York

God created the universe
and billions of galaxies within it
and millions of worlds
within them and thousands
of planets within them
and hundreds of cities upon them —
Each, God made different,
with languages and cultures
as vast as the universe is large.

And within it all, God created
one New York: A glorious
crossroad where all of creation
has a sample. And here,
in this city God said,
"Get acquainted."
And here in this city, we did.

I think God made this city
so that all of the beings of all
of the universes could have faith;
to see New York and be awe struck
by what only God could do.

Trophy Case

If all bullies did was bully
school might be tolerable.
But the bullies are loved,
treated as if they were heroes
for their strengths,
for their skills,
for their victories upon victories.
And the weird little geeks
that get kicked and pushed
are required to walk past
a trophy case
full of erections
glorifying oppressors
until one weird geek
sacrifices everything
to take a baseball bat
to a trophy case,
or an assault rifle
to a cafeteria,
or on a larger scale,
boards an airplane
and brings down
a pair of trophies
as big as the world.

Juice

On average,
the wait is two hours.
The woman who brought
orange juice
addresses me:
"You've been here before,
you can't give blood
twice in a day."
I tell her,
I slept with a man
too recently,
they won't take my blood
but I can drive
some people without transportation
to their donating appointments.
Everyone helps
however they can.
For a moment I am scared
she is going to take
my orange juice away.
I become possessive over it
as if drinking from that cup
could bring someone back.

Pythonic

New York has always been
too stubborn to admit
an injury is crippling.
We are Monty Python's knight
Yelling in The Holy Grail,
"What, that? It's just a flesh wound,
Come back and fight
you yellow bastard!"
Two arms chopped off.

Nostradamus

For all the people
who have told me
that Nostradamus
Forecasted this disaster

For all the people
who forwarded e-mails
full of the man's eerie
predictions come true

I would like to say, thank you.
I've seen and heard it now
several times, in fact
And if you knew something we didn't
you might have spoken up
the Monday before September 11th.

Our Souls

What do you think happens
to our souls after we die?
Will they feel the cold
when it snows? Will they fight
the wind as we do?
When our souls meet after life,
will they run toward eachother?
Will we have forgiven eachother
for transgressions that only matter
to the living and their lives?
Will we be able to tell eachother,
without our mouths,
how much more important
love turned out to be
than we ever thought it would?

Being Safe

A friend in Chicago
tells me over the phone
how frightened she is.
"Did you see that two more
sets of terrorists
were arrested at airports?
I don't think the last is over."
I assure her,
they will only attack symbols
of American Bravado.
"You live near Wrigley Field,
You couldn't be safer."

First Show After

Fall is a busy time.
I have back to back shows
Different city every day.
Each is a special occasion for them,
another day on the job for me.

This one is Central Park,
a little to close to the hot zone.
It's supposed to be
a Poly pride celebration
but no one is feeling very festive.

It is the first of I'm sure dozens
of events I'll be reading at
where the host orchestrates
a moment of silence
for the victims of
September 11$^{th's}$ attack
and it's aftermath.

A moment will not be sufficient.
There aren't enough moments
The silence comes too easily.

Tension

I am not interested
in the explosion
nor the blood splatters
on concrete chunks
nor the steel girders
twisted around side turned cars.

It is the ticking
that distresses me.
the ticking that may
be only a tongue's steady rhythm
against the inside of spit-slick teeth
or ticking hidden behind sheet rock
or ticking parked in a U-Haul
rented under an assumed name.

World Trade Center

With your left hand you push
a mass of dark hair off your forehead,
fingers like a rake in a Zen garden
landscaping rows that will,
in moments fall back
to being a mess in your face.

This is how I remember you.
Not as the destructive angel
who's betrayed everyone who's ever
had the misfortune to be loved by her
on her endless quest for sympathy.

We haven't been together since
the end of one disaster (ours)
since well before the start
of another (the country's)

I feel guilty for every fleeting moment
I see one as a metaphor for the other
but when I admit it to myself
these disasters ring similar.

This summer was a building
collapsing on top of me —

A lesson in how much easier it is
to hate than it is to love.

My tour. My disaster.
Oh, when I said we could do this,

I meant we could, as long as everyone
cooperates with each other, respects
each other, works together.

What was I thinking?
Selena's a drunk. Melisa,
she was The Chupacabra,
and you, you brat!
You make friends by getting people
to feel sorry for you. It worked
on me. I turned on my friend,
thinking he was making you cry.

It worked against me too.
And I trusted you so I didn't know
why my friends were disappearing
like bottle rockets, exploding
when I tried to ask. Emily, Jeanne,
Selena, Melisa. Oh Jaime
What favor did you do them
to make them think I was their enemy?

You did so much damage,
so much destruction
and your tearful apology
was so sincere
I kept forgiving you
against all reason,
I kept letting you destroy
more and more until I realized
(it was in the cab on the way
to the Cornelia Street Cafe)
you are always sorry
for what you'd lost, never
for the harm you had done.
And then it was really over.

Not even the desire to understand
could keep me with you.
I walked away not knowing
why or what or how
or if you loved me,
and I kept walking.

How ironic should it be then
that a symbol of our failure
would be the night we were
all to meet in the bar on the top
of the World Trade Center:
Windows on the World. Look at it now:
Now Windows on the Ground.

We were all coming
from different areas of the city
to the most difficult landmark
to miss and you never made it.

Our tour mates certainly showed
where their priorities are.
It took me two hours to get
one of their drunk asses out
to go claim a cell phone
from coat check to see
if you had called. Of course, you had,
and we learned they had
turned you away down stairs
for not being dressed properly.

And that was a drama too.
They didn't tell you that was why,
just fucked with you,
sending you away to the wrong place
and having a laugh about it.

I'd talked to those guys,
describing you to them.
They said nothing of it.

I wonder if they died
when the towers came down.

And if I should feel guilty
for smiling at the thought.

Later you told me
you'd have rathered
If I hadn't cared
what might have
happened to you either.
That you couldn't stand
the burden of someone's love.

I'd have worried about anyone.
And suddenly I was ashamed
of loving people of all awful things
to be ashamed of.

On the top floor of the World
Trade Center I stood, toes up
against the window and looked out
on the city. It was frightening
how high up we were.
That anything could happen
and we'd never make it
all the way down in time to get out.
But you weren't ever in the towers.
You were always above me.

I wish I knew for sure,
when the plane you were on

was crashing into my life,
if you were steering
or screaming, or both.

When I start to miss you
I well with anger enough to hurt you.
Then, when I resolve to hang up
the phone silently if you ever
call again I begin to miss you anew.

All the time I've known you
you've only treated well
people you don't love.
I liked it before you loved me.
I miss that, like I miss when you
were pushing the hair
out of your face.

I keep trying to resolve this conflict:
I miss you, I hate you,
I love you, I want to hurt you —
that one must not have resolution
or not one that I can control.
Like, what if you said you were sorry
and meant it the way I needed you to.
Would I even believe it now?

Could we recover from this disaster?
We'd have a better chance if we tried
to put the World Trade Center
back together again.

Prowl

Life has become
So unattractive
The Earth has become
A werewolf prowling
For it's next kill
The souls of the dead
Are not singing
They are screaming to us
To get away
Leave this awful place
I got away
But there was nowhere to go.

OK

We arrive at the amusement park
at ten but it takes over an hour
to find a place to put the car.
This is our first trip to Oklahoma
and we are at the state's feature attraction.
Well worth the five bucks we pay
to have our pictures taken
with the famous bomb site.

We buy a snow cone and souvenirs
from one of the gift shops on the midway:
for her, a replica of the memorial fence
complete with little pictures of the dead
and adorable, "What Would Jesus Do"
bracelets. I get a limited edition
signed and numbered Timothy
McVeigh action figure.

Off to the far right we catch a side show.
This one is called, "And Jesus Wept."
It is a monolithic statue resembling both
The Lord Jesus, and Doctor Zaus
from *Planet of the Apes*. His stone back
is aimed at the former Federal building
now astroturfed over the decimation of life
as well as some of the hope
that there could really be a loving god.

And I don't know what Jesus would do
but I am sure He wouldn't turn his back.

High Time I Say

It's taken me this long
just to get the idea
that people are really dead.
One of those people
could have been any friend,
or family, or a stranger
I might have met one day
and loved. Or you.
The next disaster
could take you from me
before I got to love you.
Think of all the people already
that I never got to love!
I don't want to wait
until I know you
to tell you how I have felt
all this time.
I love you now!
I need to tell you now.
Tomorrow may be too late,
five minutes from now
might be too late
for you to hear me tell you
and mean it, that I love you
very very much,
that you are dear to me,
all my friends, all my family,
and my strangers.

Rebecca and the Trees

Coming off the stage
I can't see through tears
although I am not sure
why I am crying
other than that I thought
I could perform my poetry
under any circumstances
and it turned out
I am much weaker
than I thought.

Someone is hugging me
Then two, then three.
One is Rebecca. I love her.
I don't know who the others are,
but I love them too.

I look past the smattering of people,
little clumps of hugs like mine
to the trees of Central Park
thinking I could learn from them
how to stand up.

Symbols

You know, the World Trade Center
is veritable symbol
of corporate America:
The force that has been ravaging
The Third World for a decade.
And the Pentagon? What is that
if not a symbol
of our arrogant waiving penis?
How often have we foolishly
thought it's burning
would be a symbol of peace?
But these are not symbolic flames.

I see anger taken beyond it's limits.
More anger than could possibly
be housed in any human body.
Like the world has risen up
a frustrated child who can stand
no more, whose tantrum
brings down steel
like it was aluminum,
concrete as though
it were library paste.
I am insistent
against all evidence otherwise,
that people are incapable
of committing offences
as horrible as this on other people.

That this is the work of symbols
enacting their rage
against other symbols
(and symbols have a way

of using innocent bystanders
as shields). I've been told
that no one is innocent.
To that, I say,
no one is that guilty.
Only our symbols
which can change meaning
in the 17 minutes
between 8:46 and 9:03
This is the United States
of America, We are Americans.
We are towers of strength.
Our towers are unrazable.

Portrait of a Girl With a Violin

Amidst it all an old man turns
and announces "There is no god
and this is proof!" As if proof
was ever needed one way
or another. I want to argue
smaller points: This is the proof?
Not AIDS? Not Hitler?
Not Hiroshima? But I say nothing
until a young woman
who has removed
a violin from it's case
begins playing.
This is her response
to the old man
who says there is no god.
I thought of speaking then,
of saying, "What's that
if not the voice of God?"
But it wasn't necessary.
The voice of God
was speaking for God.
The Young woman continued to play
and we all, even the old man,
felt the love of God engulf us.

Senses

Watch as the city's hair greys
feel the island sink underfoot
the weight of reporters,
film crews, photojournalists,
being more than can be withstood
listen for the sound
of rescue workers digging
in the rubble looking for people
finding only parts. And the sound
of a triangle announcing
one last meal before we cannot
tell the difference between
the scent of a rose and the stench
of the dead. Taste victory
where there is none to be tasted
other than what we fabricate
to make it possible to sleep.

Racks of Postcards

I was looking for a postcard
around time square, where
they are always cheap and abundant.
Rack after rack, no image
of the World Trade Center.
One clerk looks at me. I ask,
"What, a snow globe
with the Trade Center
a hundred dollar
collectors item now?"
He tells me in broken English
that merchandise has been put away
not to make a profit, but to keep
from reminding people.
"That's nice of you" I said.
It doesn't occur to me
That he was probably Pakistani.
Reminders could be dangerous.
Reminders could be deadly
and enough innocent people
have already died.

Posters of the Lost

If I had died Tuesday,
in the World Trade Center,
would you have answered
a frantic, worried e-mail
with, "I'm on my way!" —
Would you have spent
days putting posters up
with my picture on them
all over the city,
hoping beyond hope
that I, walking somewhere,
I might see it,
oblivious to what
had happened,
maybe so involved
in what I was doing
I didn't notice;
If I had not
answered my phone
to say I was fine and say,
by my tone,
that I was still
so angry at you.
If that hadn't happened,
would you be
crying on strangers,
trying not to mourn
before knowing for sure
that I had died,
holding hope like a mazāltob,
would you remember
how much you love me
if I were missing in the rubble

of The World Trade Center
rather than that I walked out
of the Cornelia Street Café,
and away from you
and away from the disaster
you made of my life.

Rilke's City

The faces in my ravaged city
wilt like the garden in 'Autumn'
with wrinkles that were not there
last month, burrowing deep,
getting comfortable
for a long stay —
No one I've seen today,
from Penn Station
to Washington Heights
put make up on,
or paid attention
while combing their hair.
It is enough that they left
their apartments at all,
those who did not
have at least the purpose
of disaster relief work.

Before the attack,
I could have met the gaze
of any one of these men
and women and thought,
potential lover, if I struck up
conversation with you,
might you, one day, love me?
Or I you?   Not now though.
Now that the bodies of strangers
have exploded to dust
so small it is carried on our air:

We've breathed in the dead
and breathed out again.
Under the circumstances,
no one looks sexy,
though everyone
looks lovable, real,
human, and grateful to be alive.

Choices

One woman who jumped
to her death, rather than
burn with the building,
landed on a firefighter.
And I hope which woman
that was will never be identified.
That her family
will remember her
as one of many who were
tragically killed, not as one
who's last decision
had her take
an extra life on her way out.

For A Book

An artist friend offers,
If I should write one,
To illustrate my book
of 911 disaster poems
Like it is difficult to draw
A pair of buildings
No longer there.

My Disaster Poem Book

Until my artist friend brought it up
I hadn't thought all these poems
could end up a book.
Now I think of little else.
Yes, I think, they could, and I could
put some of my poems
about Jaime in it, blur the line
between the world's disaster
and mine, as it is blurred to me.

That might work very well,
people who didn't know better
might think there was
no Jaime person at all,
that the love-tragedy was just
a metaphor to help
comprehend the incomprehensible
(isn't that just
what metaphors are for,
and just what poets do with them).

Yes, if I can get a publisher
to fall for it, I just might
have a book here. And if I do,
wouldn't it be just like me
to include this poem,
and give myself away.

On Leaving New York

Out of the tunnel
into Jersey
I feel the weight of a woman
next to me
on the Greyhound bus

as we turn a bend —
our eyes meet
the skyline of New York
now indistinguishable
from any other cityscape.

It was like the first time
I can remember
seeing New York's outline
from my father's station wagon
On Route to North Port Long Island
and a family occasion.
I couldn't speak,
just breathing it in.

Then in '75 when I saw it
with the addition of the new
World Trade Center
how I thought,
what a god damned monstrosity
overwhelming everything around it.

"Disgusting." I said,
if I said anything,
and I think I did.

The woman next to me
might have even been born
when the World Trade Center was built.
I'm sure she doesn't remember
a time when it wasn't there.

Despite this,
our experiences feel similar —
neither can speak —
we breath a language all it's own,
end up hugging eachother
(something we must have needed,
despite how many hugs
we've already gotten)

At no point in the trip
do we make eye contact.
We are strangers
who happened to share
the same breath.

Your Poem Somewhere

I left your poem somewhere
somewhere has your poem now

unwritten accept for a scratch
scratches on a diner napkin

read it only the once
as I wrote it expected later,
to read and write it better

when your poem
could define you to me and I could defend
myself to my poem

I committed none of it, could rewrite
none of it if demanded to.

I left somewhere without your poem
making my time somewhere with you

that much more a wasted time
wasted love, wasted somewhere

Childhood

My sister,
two years older than me
corrects my early
childhood memories,
"I'm sure it was
meaningful to you,"
she says, "but that wasn't
you and our dad,
it was Bob and Big Bird."

Recovery

It occurs to me that my efforts
have always been consumed
by working toward recovering
from one disaster or another.
I've been outnumbered
by people who have never
known hardship, looked down on
for their accomplishments
over mine, as if we had started
on a level playing field.

I look around at multitudes
who now know
what tragedy looks like
and I say, awful, isn't it?
I've never known life without it.
I know how to survive
and accomplish things
amid such disaster.
Even find moments
of peace, happiness, love.
Like Joseph, I am
sad for your misfortune
At the same time I proclaim
that in this world
I am useful. If anyone
wants to use me.

Rethinking the Crack About Calling You a Brat, Selena a Drunk and Melisa the Chupacabra

Angrily, someone
is going to ask me
How I could write
about what happened.

I've asked myself this too.
A better question would be
how could I not write about it?
This disaster profoundly
effected my life
and that is all
I ever write about.

Every pile
on the dung heap
is fair game for a poem —
anyone who didn't want
to be a poem,
shouldn't have been a shit.

Before Children

I'm standing in front
of a third grade class:
seven year olds that have been
seeing on television celebrations
in the streets of foreign countries.

One asks, "Why do they hate us?"
This is the very reason I prefer
adult audiences. Few difficult questions
and an understanding
that my answer might be wrong.

Hate, I say, is so messy,
if you use it, it gets all over everything.
I go around the circle
asking what they hate.
The consensus is spinach.
Too bad, I like spinach,
but rather than say anything,
I just go with it
not really sure where I am going
but hoping it'll make sense
by the time I get there.

Do you hate spinach so much
that you hate
the farmer that grows it?
So much that you hate
the grocer who buys it from the farmer?
So much that you hate the town
where the grocer lives too?
Do you see how hate
just spreads out?

I don't think they are getting it
when a girl raises her hand high,
holding it up with her other hand.
When called on, she announces
that she isn't going to hate
spinach anymore. "I don't enjoy
the taste of spinach," she says,
"or the smell..." (her classmates nod)
"but if someone else does,
that's ok with me. I'm glad
there is spinach for them."

She asks if that is okay.
I tell her yes, very much so.

A Plane

The first plane I see in the sky
since September 11th
is over Gary Indiana
while I'm on my Greyhound bus
I have a show in Milwaukee
in about ten hours
and I'm pretty sure I'm not
getting any sleep before doing it.

The plane appears to be
headed for Chicago.
It disturbs me like the sound
of a dentist drill.
I think how stupid I will feel
if it is terrorists
determined to take out
Wrigley field after all.

Board Games

Our rules were modified
attempts to adapt to
the missing pieces of our

Games picked up at flea markets
usually for a quarter,
never complete

We wrote exchange rates
between Monopoly
and Life play money

Drew dominoes
to count out spaces
Toward a Mystery Date

Professor Plum
could do it in the library
with a funny bone.

Insomnia

I dreamed walking naked with you
passing brownstone steps dripping
with the tears of Catholic candles
in this formerly immovable city.
We had become naked on this path
could have followed
our strewn clothing if we ever
wanted to go back to our
starting point (which we won't).

Awake, I leave my disoriented hotel
in favor of dark exterior corridors,
a newspaper blown off a stack
someone neglected
to bind before leaving out
for the recyclers
touts headline: death penalty
will be sought for teen
who's baby powder anthrax hoax
frightened a bank full of workers

My darling disaster, I miss you
so that rather than sleep alone
I am walking city streets
as four breaks into five
in the morning and I
am hoping for dawn
to come undress me.

Self-Examination

(the poem I was working on for breast cancer awareness month September 11th before I heard the news of the disaster)

It is the beginning of the month Jason stands naked in front of his bathroom mirror looking for anomalies: dimpling, scaling, enlargement first with hands on his head, then with his hands on his hips he checks his nipples to see if there's a discharge or some bleeding. If he finds nothing, like he found last month, he does not thank God yet.

Sometimes Jason begins his self-examination under the arm, moving his fingers down until they are below the breast, creeping his fingers toward the center and tracing back up, slowly, making sure to cover the entire surface in both directions.

Other times he starts at the outer edge of each breast, walks his fingers slowly around— When they are back where he started, he'll make the circle a little smaller and do it again, working his way toward the nipple.

Jason knows these two ways to do it, although he also knows there are more. Two ways is enough. He alternates them, one self-examination a month sometimes more if the fear of lumps is keeping him awake.

When he is finished with his breasts, he checks over them; under his arms around his shoulders too. This time, if he finds nothing, he thanks God.

Jason isn't checking for a lump. He's checking for another lump. Jason had a malignant lump removed from a breast two years ago. Jason is checking to see if his breast cancer has come back.

It is the beginning of the month Jason is standing naked in front of his bathroom mirror again ready to start at the top and work his way down.

The Television Will Not be Revolutionized

The Television Will Not be Revolutionized
You will not be able to download new instalments of the X-Files in six tenth of a second with computer generated actors replacing Gillian and David — you will not be able to touch a button on your remote control to see those computer generated actors basking in blue light right before your eyes because the Television will not be revolutionized
The Television Will Not be Revolutionized

Your television will not know your menstrual cycle, it will not try to sell you tampax in 28 day intervals, it will not know when your period is late and offer you an Early Pregnancy Test, your television will not know when your period is early and show you a selection of color safe bleaches guaranteed to remove stains from your favorite shorts, all sorts of hopes for space aged marketing won't be realized Because the Television will not be Revolutionized

A and E will not do a biography of Amiri Baraka, it will produce and update biographies of Maya Angelou and Shel Silverstein until we are sick to our rhyming light verse, but worse, a biography of Gil Scott-Heron will never happen, production executives will damn anyone who tries it's their job to insure that the television will not be revolutionized

No, The Television Will Not be Revolutionized
Nor will the television be revolutionary, for the people, the revolution came and went, it took place on television, but it was not the people rising, the people sat down on their sofas allowing themselves to be fed stupider and stupider programing, watching intelligence fall, watching rating rise assuring that the television will not be revolutionized

Not only have we eaten the valueless shit they sold us but we've paid for the privilege to have that shit supersized Thanks to that revolution, we don't mind at all that the television will not be revolutionized

You will never be touched by an Angel, Darma and Greg won't get divorced with a bitter custody battle, there was nothing in the 70's worth getting nostalgic over and you have no needs television doesn't pretend it satisfies so the television will not be revolutionized. Survivor 3 can be 12 Americans trying to make it a week without flicking on the tube, and they'll kill themselves rather than go through with it. You'd rather have mass produced garbage than art, real reality in all it's dirty and unpredictable glory is distasteful to you compared to the reality shows television has homogenized So the television will not be revolutionized. The Television Will Not be Revolutionized... Not be Revolutionized... Not be Revolutionized... Not be Revolutionized

Money Matters

The economy is at issue
with market strategists
on television urging
us to keep our money
in the bank
not sell stocks, go to work
and of course,
spend spend spend.
Now is the time
to invest in America,
when business is at
it's worst for everyone
accept the flag makers,
prostitutes, and undertakers.

The Pentagon

Do you think the families
Of those lost in the Pentagon
Envy the attention lavished
On those lost in New York?
Do they see the difference?
That the Pentagon
is a military target
It's employees and families
knew they were at risk.
A receptionist
in an accounting office
should not think
she might be leaving
for work to be killed.

End of Hope

It has been five days
since a survivor was pulled
from the remains
of the twin towers
though there is hope
that pockets are deeper down
where people may
be able to survive
without food or water
possibly injured
until just about now.

The Salamanders

Yesterday I waded through
a wooded Wisconsin stream,
collected mud around
my rolled pant cuffs,
lifted rocks looking for crawfish,
found instead a yellow striped
salamander — played with it
on wet leaves a game only
salamanders know the rules to.

Today I submerged my body
in lavender scented bubbles —
a bath drawn in a Des Moines hotel room
courtesy of the venue
I read my poetry in earlier that night.
I powdered myself thoroughly
and watched Queer as Folk on Showtime,
drinking green Frutopia naked
accept for a towel wrapping my wet hair
like the blue turban
of Nostradamus premonitions.

These transitions have become
normal for me. I can honestly say
I remain the same person through —
I won't say one is more comfortable,
all worlds have their comforts.

Dryer soft towels may comfort
the body but the smell of wet leaves
in Wisconsin comforts the soul —
if asked to pick I would want
the life that I have.

An ample helping of all comforts
gentle and rugged — in times
as unpredictable as these
have turned out to be
when giant towers
that stood triumphantly
over the greatest city in America
can be reduced to rubble
by a handful of zealots
with plastic knives — I am thankful
for a life that surprises me
with comforts of so many natures
and blessings as varied
as the universe is large

I am grateful to live in a world
with lavender scented bubble bath,
yellow striped salamanders
and everything in between.

Patriotism

As many as there are
Flags in windows

There are more leaves
on branches

look at them all
proudly identifying themselves

"See, here! I am a tree!"
It is late September.

Soon leaves and flags
will be coming down.

Constants

Right Wing
Religious extremists

Regardless of
what religion

Are dying
to kill people

Always in
the name of
their God

Never in
the spirit of.

Van Gogh

In Chicago 9 days
since hell came to New York
I'll be heading back shortly
but I'm stealing days
away from the destruction.

This day I've gone to see
The Van Gogh exhibition
with a sweet (if childish) young artist
I would have wanted to love
a couple of months ago
when we met her together.

Standing in front of Starry Night,
overwhelmed by it's passion,
hearing Harry Chapin's song
in my head, I wanted to pull you
toward me and kiss you
with Van Gogh's intensity.

I almost kissed the artist girl instead —
her greatest appeal now proximity —
instead, I look at the painting
and allow myself to feel
what it is to be sad.

The Sight

Two blocks from where you can see the
remains of the Trade Center
a boy has his bike overturned.
He tries a few times before getting it's chain
back on the gears.

If asked, he might tell you,
as if you didn't know about it,
"Planes crashed into those two
towers, first one, then another
and kablooie they were demolished"
using hand gestures to indicate
the scope of the fireball
as he says, 'kablooie.'

As he peddles off a woman gets
a ring from his bell (nice thumb work).
She stopped short in front
of him perhaps remembering
something she'd left in a restaurant
or on the seat of a bus.

The boy is smaller now,
two blocks further up. Where he is,
he can look up the street
and see the crews
working on the wreckage —
I see him stop and turn his head
and I know what he's looking at.

I Could, Easy

I could take my life
easier than friends
who talk about suicide
as if it were dramatic:

easy as taking
a ripe tangerine
from the vegetable crisper,
peeling the skin

away from the wedges.
Easy as running
a cool bath in summer
with a cap of bubble soap.

Easy as having too few expectations
to be disappointed. Easy as telling someone
I love that I don't
or someone I don't that I do.

Easy as getting out of bed
yet again. Easy as getting back in

and disappearing under the covers.

Yes

You had asked if I wanted you.
I didn't give you an answer
because nothing I've wanted
was ever as sweet as the best
of what I didn't know to want
that just came into my life
and I wanted whatever we had
to be sweet. When you insisted
in knowing, I said, "you're here
aren't you" believing this said
everything that needed saying.
What a lie that turned out to be.
You are not here now. I do
want you to be. Despite everything,
Yes, I want you. Yes, I do.

Love Doesn't Die

The most awful of it
is that love continues to live
a sad penumbra
reminding me how
the hands I took hold of
so freely are not my right
to hold again;
That when I lied
with my head on your belly
you could feel my heartbeat
inside your vagina.
I can't call you to read you
a poem you inspired
or tell you how much
I love sushi, and my first
taste of it was with you,
that I learned how to make it,
roll nori, pinch fish eggs,
or that I have CDs
of that band we liked together,
Or how badly I blew
my first date after you
because I couldn't suppress
love that doesn't die
even when you want it to.

Progress

The lot of them drank
Instant cappuccino, wore out
The eye piece on their
Spectron microscope,
Genetically engineered
A new strain of HIV
To use as a vaccine,
Which worked:

Made several rats
And spider monkeys
Resistant to the virus--
Couldn't get FDA approval
For tests on human subjects:
Terminal cancer patient
Volunteers. US wanted
Five more years of monkeys--

Moved the operation
To Southern India,
Tested the vaccine
On people there--
Fifty-three died. But not
From AIDS. All of
The test group, also most
Of the control group who
Had only taken sugar water.

For the "Terrorists"

If you had studied
the American culture
you would know
how persistent we are —
We will build
a Phoenix Center
that will rise from the ashes
of what you've destroyed —
Where there were two towers
soon there will be four.
Knock them down
and eight will rise
in their place — you failed!
We are not terrorized,
we are angry
and Americans use their anger,
Chanel it into productivity
to create something better
of themselves and their world.

Concession

Yes, there are destroyers
in this world.
They will continue to destroy
and I can't stop them.

They have the power to destroy
anything I can create

But I have the power to keep creating
despite what they do to my creations.

It may not be much
But that is what I resolve to do.

Every year on the grounds of Fort Benning in Columbus Georgia, The US Army trains approximately two thousand Latin American Soldiers in the art of torture and assassination. Graduates of this school have committed acts of terrorism against their Countries' civilian population and against all of humanity more heinous than any that have been committed on US soil. These acts have resulted in the deaths of hundreds of thousands of men, women, and children and include the raping of American nuns, the killing of priests, and the brazen assassination of Arch Bishop Oscar Romaro.

After reading the poems in this book, I hope you will consider that we cannot abolish terrorism as long as we are still committing it.

For more information about the effort to close the US Army's School of Assassins visit www.soaw.org

* * *

Please remember that art plays a crucial role in disaster recovery and disaster relief. I urge you to contribute to and support the non-profit arts and literary organization, *A Gathering of the Tribes*, 285 East 3rd Street New York NY 10009 www.tribes.org

Brett Axel is a peace activist, poet, and dedicated Unitarian Universalist who lives and writes in Utica, New York. His books include *First on the Fire* (A Gathering of the Tribes, 1999) and *Will Work For Peace* (Zeropanik Press, 2000).

He has given live performances of his poetry in 40 states and 8 countries including at The Bumbershoot Festival in Seattle Washington, The Off the Shelf Literary Festival in Sheffield England, Saint Marks Poetry Project in New York, NY, and The Enoch Pratt Library in Baltimore Maryland.

His poetry has appeared in *Heaven Bone, Princeton Arts Review, Algonquin Quarterly, Small Change, Long Shot, The Orange Review, Fertile Ground, The Unknown Writer, Pudding*, and *Montserrat Review*.

He has gone to Slam Nationals three consecutive years representing Woodstock, and intends to be in Minneapolis August 2002 to make it four. www.nps2002.com

E-mail Brett at axels@adelphia.net
or visit him online at: www.mybizz.net/~axels/mna.html

All rights reserved. To reprint, reproduce, or transmit electronically, or by recording all or part of Disaster Relief Poems, beyond brief excerpts for reviews or educational purposes please send a written request to the Writer's Publishing Cooperative at: W. P. C.-Minimal Press PO Box 114 Warner, NH 03278

Library of congress in publication data pending.

* * *

HongNian Zhang trained at Central Art Academy, China's most prestigious art school. He has been featured on CBS Sunday Morning show and recently completed a series of major oil paintings for National Geographic Society recreating events from ancient Chinese history. Zhang lives with his family in rural Woodstock, NY. His recent book, "The Yin-Yang of Painting" has been received with critical acclaim.

HongNian Zhang's work is available from Fletcher Galleries in Woodstock, NY

http://www.fletchergallery.com